APOLOGY OF A GIRL WHO IS
TOLD SHE IS GOING TO HELL

Apology of a Girl Who Is Told She Is Going to Hell

Poems by Devon Moore

Mayapple Press 2015

Published by   Mayapple Press
                362 Chestnut Hill Road
                Woodstock, NY 12498
                www.mayapplepress.com

ISBN: 978-1-936419-54-8
Library of Congress Control Number: 2015902738

ACKNOWLEDGMENTS

Many thanks to the editors of the following publications, in which these poems first appeared:

Cider Press Review: For Knives, Bridges, and Balconies; *Foothill:*The Lady in White is Coming Down the Stairs and Visitations; *Gulf Coast*: Red; *Harpur Palate*: Why I Return to West Avenue, Driving Down the Street Slow and The Skeleton Pier; *Ovenbird:* The Caged Girl Wishes That the Man in the Volcano Was Free Like Her; *Stone Canoe*: *A Journal of Arts, Literature, and Social Commentary*: Patricide and A Skeptic Looks Up the Brooklyn Bridge, Shivers.

Cover art, "voy a navegar la pena pa' no ahogarme en el viaje" ("I'm going to sail over sorrow so this journey doesn't drown me") by Valentina Contreras. Cover designed by Judith Kerman. Book designed and typset by Amee Schmidt with cover titles in Oaxaqueña Tall, poem titles in Gar-A-MondTall light, and text in Adobe Garamond Pro extended vertically.

Contents

For my mother, Anda Moore.

And for my father, Clifton Moore,
who told me I'd write a book one day
and left me in his will "everything unicorn."

Red

I tell you this so that you know: There was once a body
of a woman on the beach, with legs glowing white and the fabric

of her bathing suit bodice strained. I yelled *mother* at her
from the water of a lake, my tiptoes barely puncturing the sand bottom,

my neck barely reaching air. I wanted her to float with me,
be as I was, a suspended tensile weight. In that position

there was no need for food or shelter, there would be no need
for imagining things. In that position, there was that feeling that

you could be all the things you weren't, but she wouldn't come,
wouldn't even look at my voice directed at her across the slow

rolling Erie, wouldn't even look when the life guard jumped in
to save me. Shame, the kind caused by going to school with stains

on your sweatpants, the same shirt for a month, for a year,
sticks to your ribs like fat. We teach ourselves shame

of our fat and breasts and muscles, too. My mother and I, little girls
decades apart, keep walking outside of ourselves to get away.

She was once a girl in a red dress, bony armed, wrists
you could wrap a fist around, a chest of rosebuds, and a pile of adventure

books by the bed she shared with her sister and all that a lit cigarette
against her skin would later fail to deliver. For a day my mother had

a new red dress, so pretty, so pretty, all other desired redresses
of poverty and drunkenness forgotten for that tensile moment,

she floated in happiness when she set the dress in the bathtub,
poured out the bleach to clean it, a corrosiveness at hand

she didn't recognize until too late. I tell you this so that you know:
there are some absences of color I can't get back for her,

5

even when I write *red* and *red* and *red* and *red*, even when I call
out to her, *mother*, my voice pummeling through the silver

prismatic light reflected on a lake, her body,
moving slow and so far away.

Remembering Why I Wanted to Be Human

In the morning, I'm at the table.
The scientists in a magazine have me wondering
about toddlers and the acceptable amount of arsenic
in a sippy-cup full of apple juice.
And an artist is saying his process of working is to figure out
how to survive life. I'm trying to look at myself as I am,
but the past has two faces,
golden and ungolden.
We were suffering
from a fissure, people who have fallen out of love sometimes
guillotine one another,
and your mother collects empty houses
because they're safer. We don't need heads
for this kind of loneliness, but the sculptor in the magazine says she needs
her memories,
they are her documents.

I never told you about when
on the back porch the woman who claimed to be psychic
said remember why you wanted to be human
said she could see my art everywhere, in the air
said star child, you have many exits.

Trying to remember why, I am lonelier than winter.
When I first met your mother, deaf from birth,
I remember thinking you had two names,
the one I would say and the sound of your name wrenching
from her throat, a shadow of another
world, the phonetics of mouth motion, the guttural,
the, to her, unheard.

She lined her empty houses out on shelves
and turned on the lighthouse lights.
I've been wondering about the shapes my thoughts make,
how I articulate them to myself in words, in sound,
in questions, what form do her thoughts take?
What would my lips communicate to her if she read them now?

I wish I was there with you,
moving the world outside the windows.
Do you have my memories?
All I want to know is
where the ground is.
Who your mother is.
Will you come back, love.

For Knives, Bridges, and Balconies

The pears I bought and put in the glass bowl are cinnamon stick red
and rough. Pleasurable it is, the cutting them up and the looking.

Question: What couldn't you help but do in a room where one wall
is a window? Answer: See all the other rooms you're not in.

The improbability of probability is a law we know. One day it snowed,
it hailed, it rained, but we were surprised when the sun shone.

Once you slept in a hotel room next to a balcony
and the back of your soon-to-be-ex-lover was a ledge. You are still

backing away.

All this pathos looks the same. Even if she's not
the one who jumped off a bridge, she is.

Inside the House with the Upside Down V-shaped Roof

This much is figured out: the thing about being a girl is that stuff is stuck inside you—but with a boy, stuff goes away and never comes back.
—Gary Lutz

The sun is shining particularly bright on all that the girl is keeping.
Hands stained purple with onions, a mustard seed hanging about a neck,
the black and white cat with loose-jointed limbs that can't stop falling.
How we lumber, she lumbers. The mythology of light, the cracks
in the walls. Is he home? Or was that her own voice, catching?
There's a twenty-minute walk to the door next door and a reason
why anyone would want to go there. There are tunnels under the ground
carrying water to the spaces in a cup, and veins above the ground
stretching through the leaves. Red and gold piles up, over the bodies
of last year's cats out back. Grey. Trying to sleep, but can't,
trying to close the inside eye, but can't.
It's the one that wants and wants, collects and lines it all up.
Jars of pennies, pastoral settings on stones, grease sputtering on a stove,
boxes of plastic figurines made to play war, made to play house.

In an unmade bed, I am not alone
when the wind pushes the locust tree up to the window
and shows me an unfurling face,
a face that motions more than wind,
a face that shows me more than the space available
to affix the countenance of a girl,
close-lipped, eye-lidded, and stuck.

A Word a Person Couldn't Know

She was a person, even when she was three. She was a person, even when she climbed to the roof. She was never a lonely girl, she had a head with many rooms, the way honeycomb works. When the man who was her father stood under the umbrella, the ground caught the dry space and only some of the grass turned to gold. Somebody else called it brown and said dead. She wasn't wearing ruby slippers, but she wanted to be. She wasn't wading in the brown-leather cowboy boots her father wore to the funeral home's furnace, but she wanted to be. When his bones went dust, what that part of her wanted most was to scream real loud a word a person couldn't know...

Can't think of another way to say resurrection than to say resurrection, can't think of another way to say please and don't die than to say that fire must get real hot, those bones, hard like coral, must get real soft and that girl must get real sad. These words are for the immaculate grief kept in a room by a rooftop and this wish is for the person inside who keeps drawing herself with chalk; the shapes are: legless and ruby-slippered.

The Caged Girl Wishes that the Man in the Volcano Was Free like Her

At the carnival there are stuffed fabric chupacabra dolls
and jars filled with six-footed pigs, but I am most afraid
of the man and the body of the man and the head of the group
of men that thought it was a good idea that people pay
two dollars to see this. This is not about the economy,
this is about how I bought and sold myself for a feeling
deep down in the pit of my guilt that says you enjoyed it,
you enjoyed it, and I swallowed fire like a geek does
and this isn't high school anymore. But I can't stop staring
at the alligatorturtle hybrid that I saw move, I saw move,
in a kiddie pool filled with pennies and dimes and the occasional
quarter sunk to the bottom and I'm so worried that the metal alloy
is leaching into its reptilian skin and I know that the part
alligator part turtle would be hunched in the corner if there was room
enough for a corner, and we all know that people have been visiting
his body all day to wish that they'd get laid. Or that their fathers wouldn't die.
Or that their ex-lovers would or would not get a blade to the eye.
Or that they'd come back to them and beg for forgiveness.
After a lifetime of wishing on my imperfections, on my not
too taut belly, on my slightly smaller right eye, on my less full
left breast, on the reptilian part of my brain that feels too much
too often like I should be running away down
into the bottom of the pickling jar of what went wrong.
I feel a heart. I feel a dime. I watch the creature move
as I move forward in the perpetual tunnel before a parade of eyes.

Exhibit

In a little cubby
sits a black stone sculpture.

I glimpsed its form
when the Staff Only door swung open,
but there wasn't enough time to see.

I can tell you that it was the size of a grown man's
head, or a cabbage and a half.
But it wasn't a head or a cabbage.

After we said our goodbyes
and walked away,
you towards the photography,
me towards the oil and charcoal,
I turned,
and waited for your eyes.

When you didn't look back,
I saw your black-coated figure get smaller
and farther,
until the back of your head became indistinguishable to me
from the moving heads of all the other men.

I thought, how lonely it must be
to be a black stone
sculpture in a museum
but not on display.

To be an exhibit
(of longing
or of love)
but to be this unseen.

Voice Next to the Old Shoebox from Before I Met You

I crookedly assembled myself once,
with the help of somebody else.
Watch your fingertips so they do
not get caught on the nail that is left
hanging out—ask me to look
at you, but I can't because I am
too ashamed to tell you that I am not
what I am, that these days I play
at being sure, but my hair is longer
than it once was, and tomorrow I may
cut it or I may not. I may throw
out the shoebox or I may not.
I may let you hold me
or I may not.

Anti-Sonnet

The chupacabra may just be a coyote with a demodectic mange
killing goats in Texas, but I'm more interested in the other possibility.
Perhaps this whole sucking blood thing is a big misunderstanding.
The chupacabra's skin, leathered and scaly, is really just its armor
against pain, just as the armor of these calluses along the soles of my feet,
the palms of my hands, and in the spaces between my heart and my eyes

are my own hard shells. As a child I crushed a dead wasp carcass beneath
my heel. I tried to feel nothing but the brittle give of hardened wings.
Now, for months, I sleep in an attic, a thin door between boxes
of storage and myself, a thicker door still leading in and out.
Yesterday I opened
a window in the shape of a coffin
and told a man I loved him.
Today I'm not so sure.

Swans and Geese

Whether the bees have thoughts, we cannot say.
—Roethke

I saw a goose, but inexperienced
with such things, thought I saw a swan.
It was enough that it had such a delicate,
draped down neck. Its feathers were on the grassy,
muddy shore of the pond—feathers and leaves,

feathers and leaves. After the movement
of October, the gold and red leaves smelled
of rot. I don't know much about decomposition,
only what I know about death, which is
that sometimes being in love with it is a kind

of living. I still dial the numbers of the dead man
in my sleep. I still wait for the man who is alive
to call me *love*—whether the geese who look
like swans in the pond have thoughts, I cannot
say—but the leaves, gold and red, looked at me

wrong before they fell. *Your happiness*, the man
who is alive said, *was a mirror that reflected back to me*
my own absence, so I wanted to break it. No, that is not
what he said, but what was meant. What he really said was *space,*
there is a need for space and so I pointed out the rays

in the pink and orange sky, and how we were covered
by a dome of pink and orange light. This is a geometry problem now
and I am calculating our circumference, how long it will take
for me to get from here to him. But my mind is walking upside
down around a prism that resembles a pond, while his ghost is

roaming about on a flat plane. All the buffalo are
gone, long ago, killed off by moving trains and bullets.
But their absence is a presence and I wonder if they drank
here while I wait for the freeze and the pond to solidify,
just an inch or two, so that I can meet that man again

on the polygonal surface. But the geese that are not swans
will be gone by then, and so will the feathers and the leaves, and everything
I wanted to say. I hear that geese migrate to warmer climates while
swans are supposed to stick around, if there is enough water—
I've been wondering where I'd go if I wasn't tied here,
if this space wasn't enough to keep me contained.

Let me diagram for you the pond, the feathers, the geese,
the swans, the leaves, the buffalos and their ghosts. It's the way I run
around it all, the hundreds of steps all this space takes, that makes
my ears ache from the wind. Hush, I hear a sound. I don't hear the singing
of a swan's wing, I don't hear a phone ring.

Why I Return to West Avenue, Driving down the Street Slow

Everywhere I look is an eight ball and slanting green felt-covered slate, the future I daydreamed, the bull I rode down to the river, the barrel over the falls, the length of a finger and a thumb, wrapped around a wrist. The way tape works.

Everything I taste is a heart, is the mother I would have killed, is the bed the girl burned, is the eyes I closed and closed, the queen of spades, the card of the sun, is what I turned over under the dark closet eyesight and the cigarette's glow. The skeleton baby brother I talked to in the toilet. The stories I wrote. There was the dancing in the bedroom and the baseball in the kitchen, the lamp I didn't break, the teeth that broke out, the home alone, the mother I saw cry, her resurrection, the stab, the way I hear everything. Don't listen. Don't listen. Don't leave well enough alone.

Everything my mouth reaches for is a blister, the arm of the candelabra that fell off when it got too hot and everything I don't hear is the rosebuds in the bathtub with the clawed feet, the water too hot, how I keep taking my foot out and putting it back in, taking my foot out and putting it back in, the dial tone and deep breaths. How the cold bruises the lungs and the way the snow accumulates around a tire. We dig. We dig. The building next door that burned down, the black spot, the girl who drowned with flowers, the alphabet and elements taped to a wall, a tongue mouthing zinc; two palms, cupping a pink-yellow heart, steering a wheel, tasting sweet.

Not So Anonymous

By age eight, I could not count the number of times
my mother hid me by the Bavarian cream and jelly donuts
with a box of crayons and blank paper and told me to sit still.
I reached with pudgy fingers for the bright colors and sweets
of the AA meetings and learned to keep quiet.

But what I saw on the walls of the churches' basements
were vestiges of other children's innocence
surrounding the Anonymous and me,
how cozy those crookedly finger-
painted two-dimensional walled homes seemed then,

so inviting was Noah's ark
drawn like a half-moon,
that the Anonymous never stopped to think
how the dove came bearing hope
only after the genocide of the wicked,
how if the rain fell today,
they would still be treading water
and coughing up salt and blood

and I knew how many seconds it takes to get your stomach pumped
because Earl G. told me,

and I knew the sound a fist makes
when it perforates a glass door
because Bob B., my mom's boyfriend, showed me,

and I knew how lonely silence could be
in a phone booth on Christmas Eve,
because Kathy C., who hadn't spoken to her own daughter
for three years, two months and twenty-one days,
looked at me and said nothing.

While some children tore off the gold
ribbons on Christmas gifts
or dissected their Nintendoes to see
how the little Mario man jumped,

I wanted nothing more than to unwrap the Anonymous,
to take them apart
layer of epidermis
by layer of epidermis,
to expose them from the inside,
for truth (even if they deny it),
must exist in the body if nowhere else.

So I used my own crayons and drew them surviving,
not in houses with picket fences nor in mythological boats,
but always their bone frames first,
their stomachs, their fists, their eyes,
all of Crayola's sixty-four colors blended to mud.

Later, when my mother told me
to forget them, to be a child again,
I tried to erase their bodies
and draw only rainbows,
as though such a thing were possible.

Going to Ocean

The possibility of rip currents is highest at low tide.
Here I am, at low tide, supposedly trying to avoid
rip currents. If I say to the man who used to love me, current,
he hears currant, a tiny seeded red berry too sour to eat raw,
but I am talking here of the hand
the ocean sends to bring back from the shore
all that it needs. Today the ocean doesn't need me.
Harbinger, messenger, this body in salt and sand.
My feet raked smooth. This is the truth: There are people
everywhere and I am alone. This is another truth:
There is a wave out there that is not yet a wave.
There is a force in me that is not yet a current.
The man who used to love me is in another city
and when he phones me on the digital telephone it is to say
he doesn't do long distance. He has needs, he says. I know this
to be true: Somewhere up north there are currants
glowing red in a bowl and, in the distance
of one wrist, a cup of sugar.
The sign says: If taken, swim parallel to the shore.

Explaining Loneliness in a Basement

You are there already with dirty,
dirty bare feet on cold concrete.
Forgotten was the bag of mutton bones
chewed clean by the teeth of a past love
resting in the freezer. Loneliness is the knowing
that there once was an intention
for a slow simmering soup, but forgetfulness is not
the antidote to loneliness as one might believe.
That is what the basement of our imagination is for.
Here it is easy to remember somebody else's floor
is sometimes your ceiling,
that somebody else's child's
chalk marks in the sunless shade
of a cellar corner
are sometimes doors
to other worlds.

Presence

Before my next move, in a small box
that once housed mandarin orange scented soap,
in a drawer, in a room that I have spent these last
two years walking through, I found a scrap of paper.
Small treasure, my father's scrawled hand,
a phone number he gave me years ago of a friend,
a friend he loved who he thought I could love too.
I could use a friend. I could use a father.
I could use, not just the sound of a hand knocking
on a wall, but a palm to press my fingers in
and a room to sit in for a while. Scrap of paper
in my pocket, the handwriting of the dead.

Here's to hoping that the feeling I'm being watched is real.
Here's to hoping that I wake up in my next home
to the smell of oranges, to fresh ink, to a hand
pressing a receiver to my chin, a voice in my ear.

My Father Wishes for Death

He said, "Those who were smiling died," and I expected them
to disintegrate off the pages when my father spoke,
but their bodies were forever encased by the edges
of curled up yellow paper in his old photo album.
And my dad pointed to the blond guy with freckles,
he died while being hugged by a Bouncing Betty.
It blew off his balls and his "motherfucking" head.
They called the dead blond Sunny, 'cause he was from the land
of bright orange fruit and light. He didn't have a last name,
'cause none of them did.

"It's dangerous to know more information than necessary,"
that's what my dad says, 'cause that would make them real,
not just a generation of useless John Waynes.
So they remained images in my father's mind,
more real now in his nightmares than their faces which men and metal
ripped away. There must be no more sunshine in Sunny's face,
hollowed out and sunken down. "He had no right to be smiling,"
my father said, but light shines through
even the bullet holes.

They called my father Moe.
If he had died they wouldn't have known him at all,
yet they would have known him better than anybody.
Moe pulled out his arms from underneath the bed:
a black case of guns and a knife, one side jagged, the other sharp and smooth.
He showed me how to use it.
Slice downward into the gut with the smooth edge,
then rip upward, the jagged edge tearing
the organs out through the open space.
When I asked him if he ever used it on anybody,
he said, "That's none of your business," but I knew the answer was yes.

Moe says we're all dying, right from the moment of birth.
"Shit happens and then you die" is his mantra,
and he wishes for death, while I wish he would stay.
I want him to forget he's dying, but he holds on to it like hope.

He wants the peace of death, yet not enough to be a "yellow-bellied sissy"
and do it himself, so he inhales black tar, works fourteen hour days,
crawls under houses in search of electrical currents,
and cuts his fingers off with saws.

When he's dead, he wants me to throw his body in a ditch.
He wants his body eaten by rats and white translucent worms.
No pine boxes, no quick release in the flames.
He says, "No funeral, only a big party and lots of jokes,"
but his unsmiling eyes reveal his lie. He wants me to cry for him,
he wants me to write this poem for him,
and he wants me to know him,
but not too well.

All this Dead Stuff We Have Left

If I were to get on the train and go, you and I would be okay.

Okay is something, the self-help guru says, we need to be within ourselves.

Ourselves was a state we lost, lost in the disenchantment of the attachment of us to us.

We are two people standing on a platform, watching one another wave goodbye.

We move our lips to say love and ask with our eyes: Are there windows where you are going? And having gotten there, will you continue to see only your own face and not the world's? Will you continue to think that all this loneliness you hear is not your own voice?

The world is a dish of missing knick-knack heads, heading towards the edge of the counter.

In some parts of the world, they eat the body parts of their enemies. There is part of me that would like to go there, there is a part of me that thinks we're already there, there are other parts of me I have yet to show anyone, including myself.

And my face, observed counter-clockwise, is one I don't recognize from last year's pictures or today's.

If you counter my argument that you and I are not meant for each other with pressing me down into the bed, I might believe you.

You could act like you mean it this time, and stop propping your body up against the side of the room, against the side of my eyes, stop holding yourself with caution while you reach for the dream you had in the back of your head.

It went like this: When I lost my leg, I was reaching for you while simultaneously holding onto the train. Hypocritical, I know.

Due to these circumstances, the circumstances of having an amputated leg, I am developing a ghost.

A ghost of a feeling that says to chase the bullet-moving night-train, chase down my head, follow my hands and leave you a leg.

Here it is: A ghost of a leg that says I need. You, I need you to walk away now.

Apology of a Girl Who Is Told She Is Going to Hell

I knew a woman who was born again.
She spoke in tongues on altars and planted
pink and red Impatiens in window boxes.
She said she was planting Impatiens with me
because I was an impatient child. The things

I don't touch: orange flowers on the shelf, wind chimes
that sound like bells, a brown woolly caterpillar
immobile on the cement. *Fear fear, go away,*
come again some other day. Brave,

I asked the woman what it sounded like to talk in tongues,
what it felt like to be taken over by the holy ghost,
she said no to sharing the sound of the sacred
and no to calling a cut a boo-boo
when I opened up my fingertip with the pointed end of a spade.

Let the light in, the platelets out,
this is the way pain moves both ways and words like God flow out...

She said, *no, little girl, you're doing it again,*
using God's name in vain, she said,
I will never tell you what the rapture feels like,
even what God's voice sounds like when you ask...

I imagined it sounds like the thing you say to make the hurt stop,
like child's talk, like boo-boo, like I love you,

like overflowing flowerboxes and a cat tongue
rough against your hand, how holding one red petal

feels like lying in a meadow of bloom,
one rising drop of blood smells like earth,

followed by another drop, drip, drip, drop,
but barely hurt, drop, she said, *No.*

It's called a cut, say cut, say you're sorry, say you
didn't mean boo-boo, you meant cut, say cut.

The dirt was dark, healthy looking,
like a place one could go to heal awhile…

I dipped my fingertips beneath the pink
and red buds, beneath the broad green leaves,
and felt the fluting of the roots, saying the prayer
of a child who has been told she is going to hell:

I'm sorry, I didn't mean to say God, I meant cut,
I didn't mean I love you, I meant cut,
I didn't mean to put my finger on this
vein, I meant cut.

Gardening with Gravity

I was surprised to see the red
tinting its way over the green

on the plump little tomatoes.
Do you remember how we planted it,

I thought, too late? Cross-legged
on the asphalt porch, hands in bagged

dirt and Miracle Gro, we stuffed
the Topsy Turvy planter full of black

sod and seedlings, promising each
other that they would grow, upside

down, shooting back into the direction
of the underearth and not towards the sun.

Gardening with gravity is not
as difficult as it may seem, it's natural,

you know, both wanting and not wanting
to see what's beneath the surface,

but mostly we want.
Isn't that why we flirted

in a speeding car at night, or broke the sheet
of moonlighted lake with our bodies?

I wrapped my legs around yours then
to avoid the seaweed that we couldn't

see. What you remember most is that part:
where you lifted me, joked that the lake

was a threshold and that you'd carry me
through to a honeymoon in Canada.

It got cold and what I didn't mention
was the seaweed between my toes,

or the rocks that cut my feet on the way
out, or how on the day we planted tomatoes,

the asphalt hurt my bare ankles
with its jagged black-glinting surface,

driving its impression
scary close to the bone.

This Is Your Warning

I try not to be crazy.
Sometimes I fail.
Like when I contemplated reading you
a warning, Neruda's "If You Forget Me,"
to be exact, because I felt that loving
you made me vulnerable as a hawk
tethered to a boat, buoyant and shackled,
out of flight and on water,
my talons sharp, my beak sharper,
frantically beating my wings against the bow.
I wanted a way out, so I was gnawing
on what looked like a rope
but what might have been your skin.
In this state, nothing makes sense.
I said (all Neruda-esque), "we are a floating boat,"
and I thought I heard you say, "no,
we are more than that, we are metal
and water and air," but I had lost my mind
and couldn't be sure.

And when you didn't keep your promise,
and came over at 10 instead of 8,
I thought that you had forgotten me.
and the surge of violence I felt scared me,
because I was not a hawk, we were not a boat,
and this was not a Neruda poem.
No, we were two people in a room
wearing exercise clothes, and I, still
angry, trying not to be crazy, said "I want
to uproot one of your chest hairs."
"Do it," you said, and when I plucked a black
coarse strand out of its puckered pore,
I saw in your eyes that I had hurt you,
but it wasn't enough,
so I took off my shirt and then my bra.
You said "milky" and "white," I said "don't touch,"

and I fastened my heart rate monitor's strap
beneath my breasts, licking each electrode
moist. "This is your warning," I said
as I handed you the digital watch, "77?" you read.
"Yes," I nodded, "It's barely beating for you."

A Skeptic Looks up the Brooklyn Bridge, Shivers

*Don't believe any figure that says how many feet of the bridge deck is
over the river. The actual number varies with the tide and the amount
of water coming down the Hudson River.*
—www.glasssteelandstone.com

Don't believe him when he says *yes* to love *or my favorite food
is macaroni and cheese.* Because he lied once, he is no longer

a trusted source. Don't believe the online expert when he tells you
what not to believe, when he tells you that the bridge you walked across
with the man you can no longer trust is over the Hudson, and not
the East River.
                                                            Be careful,
the man you can no longer trust said, when you were standing midway
on the centerline of the suspension bridge, a toe hovering over nothing

and the rest of you planted on a wooden plank. You thought of snapping
cords and horror movies. The man you can no longer trust stopped

thinking of romance and thought instead of your faux leather purse,
imagined its thin straps breaking, and the weighty body of it, much heavier
than you would expect from something so small, falling down

into the traffic below. *The possibilities for disaster are endless,*
the man you can no longer trust said. You and he imagine the red

car swerving to avoid it, the ensuing jolt of metal
            upon metal, bone upon bone. The whole bridge shivering

under the impact of it.
                        We didn't have time to brace our bodies
for the movement of the world and ourselves. I would later

look up the difference between tendons and ligaments
because there was an unexplained pain in my back

and the metaphoric possibilities linking cables to a bridge
that extended out like a spine were too tempting, especially after

the end of our love. We both,
the man I can no longer trust and I, had unfinished business

with the dead, having held our own dead once. Years ago,
I clipped my father's hair and wrapped it in tissue,
put the lock in a baggy and carried it around,
while the man I can no longer trust hitched rides

across the continent to get away from his brother's bones,
marrow and cancer filled. The two brothers' bodies went missing

from the bed they once shared. *We handle the dead differently
where I'm from*, said the man I can no longer trust on the bridge,

*we lay out the bodies and display them for days to allow for travel,
for visitors.* And I wanted to say I didn't

see much difference between the way he hitched a ride
on a semi and I escaped the tension in my mind,
daydreaming myself loved and far away.

We were both runaways
looking for a way out.

Consider the engineering here.
Consider the men who died down there, building it,
the air bubbles moving through their joints.

Decompression sickness is a bitch, I told the man
I had stopped trusting because there was nothing left to say.

The difference between tendons and ligaments
was the kind of unknowing that bothered me,

so I looked it up. Both link to bone, but one to muscle and the other
directly to another bone or organ. And both, I learned, are capable
of withstanding tension, to an extent,
before the pain and the breaking.

The Conversation Falls Back

We gained an hour and I lost
a lover over waffles. Time to talk,
we halved and quartered up the butter-
milk discs with the sides of our forks—
We dismantled, disseminated and
chewed those doughy dimpled circular
surfaces—He said: Intensity. I said:
Indifference. This: was sharing. I half-smiled
midway through the break-up talk, but the voice
of my inner critic spoke up—Told me: Break it.

Told me: You don't know what's best—
Told me: You are
ugly as snow after a day of mud
and thaw and horse shit. Told me:
Nobody's gonna want you after this.

Told me: Alone,
alone, that's who you are.

Outside the waffle place
I digested and walked, with only one
look back—His hunched over
hooded figure got
smaller,
so quickly.

My hands, cold,
holding nothing,

if I could I would have
gloved them.

The Pietà in Reverse

Aged nine, my father fell and was dragged
by his uncle's mail track for some distance
over gravel. Until he died, many years later
after two tours in Vietnam, two daughters
whom he loved and always missed,
too many times falling through the sky
to count, the upward rush of trees and sky,
the violent pull back of air in a parachute,
even then the scars tracked his back.

The story goes, he lost his memory,
his ability to eat and walk,
he even had to relearn to love
his own mother. The story goes
that after three weeks in a coma he woke up,
but wasn't brain damaged as expected,
he just screamed out *mama*
and struggled to get free.

What was most wondered at
is how strange it was that he had known
to cry for her, but didn't recognize that it was his
mother holding him while he cried, didn't recognize that
she was saying *I am here*, that she loved him,
that he loved her.

It was the Pietà in reverse,
a struggling to come-alive-again-dead-son,
and a mother palming back what was left
of his hair from his stitched forehead,
the same shade of black as hers.

And They Say That Cats Always Land on Their Feet

In nineteen ninety-six, in deep sleep
the black and white cat rolled off the TV
and busted both its back legs

Charlie watched as the cat
used its front legs to drag itself
in the direction of the window.
It didn't get very far.
It was a fat cat.

Splayed out behind it were the irregular shapes
that broken bones make.

Charlie ran barefoot on asphalt and gray rocks
down Lafayette Avenue to find his mama.
She was gone.

He came back bleeding. There was glass in his foot.
The cat had stopped trying.
There was no phone. Someone had not paid the bill.
Charlie and the cat looked at each other.

For the Lost

Fragile white bone china upon a shelf;
there is a crack
through the rosebud
on the Okinawan saucer
and a space
for the lost
tea cup.

Barcelona in May

My eyes down, our last day, my love had not
looked at me for hours, so I pointed out to him
that my toenails, bared whole, were painted red
in open toes, rounded at the tips, so shiny
they looked wet. "How about I be your matador,"
I half-laughed, thinking how unclever it all was,
the association between horns and cock, the trip
we had taken across the sea, as though the cobblestones
and rising spires could save us. Then pretense stopped,
my eyes darting from the Mediterranean, to the arena,
to the pebbles in the concrete.
"You know, it's always going to be like this,"
he said, "I'm always going to look through you,"
and he felt better.

Somewhere else in Spain, that same day,
a goring happened:
the bull's horn went up, straight through
the matador's neck and out of his mouth.
And there were witnesses:
an entertained crowd, a camera crew,
a victorious bull, and later, hours
of surgeons' hands and threads,
moving to needle close
a matador's open throat.

Narcissism and Stars

In the parking lot after the twelve-step meeting we stood,
tipping our chins to the sky. There were two bright stars,
brighter than those I had seen before. I asked the others,
"What is that?" One man uncraned his neck to say,
Jupiter and Venus, he knew because he studied
constellation maps, and then another man said no, Mars –
they continued to disagree, but I was thinking of satellites
and airplanes, of the constant movement
of recorded transmissions, of how all this energy can be
neither created nor destroyed, just shifted.

Alone at night I used to listen to the primordial
sounds of the galaxy on the internet,
each electrical storm of the Sun sounding just like static—
the revolution of Saturn, intermittent hisses.

I read once that when you speed up the human voice eight times,
we sound like crickets, speed it down and we transmit the ocean.

Earlier that night the topic had been surrendering
to a higher power and when it was my turn to share, I shook
my head. I want to say that I thought, *Tonight, I'm listening*,
but there is so much I don't recognize
about myself that I need to say—
such strange unidentifiable flecks
of light shining through.

After Driving Wildly to a
Watermelon Patch One Summer

When you say, *I don't drink* he smiles his sun-licked face,
smiles like he sees you. Calls you, *a good Christian girl,*

a good Christian girl tallying up these body parts that matter
to you so little. Focus on his eyelash, a dimple. Desire. Feel none.

Hair: is blonde, maybe brown, maybe blue-eyed or green. He has
a North Carolinian farm boy voice, deceptive as a bedtime

story. You mouth *fuck off* in your brain and he pours you
a glass. Three-quarters vodka. One-quarter orange juice.

Contemplate the vodka. The volume and viscosity. Whether or not
it would burn off his face if you doused him and set it on fire.

Contemplate your lack of Christianity, except that one time,
aged eight, when you laid your hands upon the TV. Think,

who could blame you? Home alone for three days and only four channels.
There was transcendence being offered in the antenna that day.

Think about the watermelon body you left in the bed of his truck.
The big black seeds. The red flesh. The white rind. Think about your own

body. How it ripened before you were ready. How there are never enough
layers to cover you up. Think about his mother in the other room. Drunk

in a housedress. How she didn't even look up when you first walked in.
When your body blocked the sitcom lights moving on her face, when you said *hello.*

Good Christian girl, he coos. His vodka breath on your neck,
and for the second time in your life, you wish that it were true.

There Must Be a Chain

Woke up to a ghost of Montreal and the last survivor of the sunken ship
following me. Witness. It had the face of a moon. I don't know

how to speak French, I don't know how to speak French. There are angels
in the shape of people at the counter serving coffee and tea, there is the raised

voice in me of a man who once told me, *you are nothing*.
His voice is still reverberating.

I have a halo inside, or a feeling that is the shape
of a halo inside. A circle is an infinite concept, yet a chain

is a series of circles with a beginning and an end. There must be a chain
connecting the moon to the window of the room I abide in,

a series of circles chaining the halos in my eyes to the craters
we sometimes mistake for the moon's eyes, my mouth making an

O, Ask yourself why, why else would the moon stay, but chains?
Why else would the moon look in to see the look on our faces when we are

told we are *nothing*, nothing but immaculate repetitions of our imperfections?
I sometimes walk away on air, sometimes on cobblestones.

If the moon were to start to leave, some
scientists would say *dead*, some

romantics would say *no*, some tides
would say *rise*, some waves

would say *stop*, some earth would say
implode, some person who is sometimes

an angel would say in song, *stay now, glow,*
you are the antidote to the burning sun.

The Lady in White Is Coming down the Stairs

These evenings I know we will die here,
eventually and aglow, reaching for pixels,

and gripping the empty bottle on the seat like the peanut shells
we busted open and found empty in our dreams.

These evenings, turning around the same
bend, the same television, the same glow.

Do you know we could have been the heroes, could have risen
up and rescued ourselves? Supposedly,

we love it here, we love the grey fleck
in the blue eye of the television star, wishing we could see

perfect like that. The heroes on the television are running
into houses and the vampire queen is chopping off their heads

with only one fingernail. We were born unflinching,
watching broken bones push through skin.

Call it anesthetization. Call it evolution. Call it
what it is. The heroes on the television have survived us,

are the fittest, are swimming over seas of our foolishly closed eyes
and calling them lakes. Real ghosts

exist, you know. I saw the lady in white, a long time ago,
in another movie, gliding down the stairs,

and in my most susceptible moments I see her again,
and close my eyes to transmit her away.

But what would she say if she could?
You were real.

You were the sound you thought you heard at the back of your head
whispering to the part of you that still listens to the truth.

Grey matter. Adjusting eye. This is not right. Look up.
See a pockmarked face. Call it a moon.

Do you know that the white matter in your bones is made
from the same calcium as those stars?

Do you know that, all along,
it's been your own light that you've been
turning off?

How scary, how easy it is,
to forget what we need
to protect ourselves from.

Failing Kindergarten

I didn't learn to read and write
like I was supposed to,
one cursive letter at a time,
in a pad of newsprint, between
two lines. The "a" must have been
curled at the end and laminated
on the wall. There must have been
a picture of a shiny red apple,
and the teacher's eyes, disapproving,
must have been descending. But I was glassless,
and could not yet see the world
internalized through a teacher's mind.

The news got out
that I didn't know the loopy
letter of the day. The teacher spoke
to my mother, told her to come in.
The verdict: her daughter was
slow. After the ride back home,
my mother cried on the brown couch
behind the closed door.

I went outside to play
beneath the crab apple trees
and daydreamed myself a super hero
for an afternoon. It was a windy day.
I wished for a kite, to feel
its tug, to guide it through
the air. Although I had never held
one, I could imagine what
it would be like, its lift and the pull –
I could feel myself leaving a world
where the contemplation of kites
was enough.

That night I sat in bed waiting for my mother
with my face in a book, looking at my favorite image:
the pink icing on the birthday cake, the yellow

candles on top, the three kittens in blue jeans,
and the printed letters beneath
that told me the kittens had made it
to surprise their mother when she came home
from work. Their mother smiled despite the mess,
and I held onto the surprise and smile so much,
the page was falling out.

Alexander Hamilton Was Killed in a Duel

and the church we were in was next to a graveyard.

Knowing this shouldn't surprise anyone.
For the same reason a tiny girl pushing her finger
into a candle flame besides a pew shouldn't
surprise anyone. It is about closeness to what hurts us

most, it's about wanting to be the one person
that death missed. And so, sometimes people pray
like that. In a town, bending towards a grave
that is my grandfather's, I brushed away

a brown folded leaf and found a disheveled looking
president on a ten dollar bill. I don't know the faces
of presidents like I should. I don't remember
my grandfather like I should.

For a day I went around showing the ten-dollar bill
to everyone I met—the porcelain doll
on my grandma's shelf, the toothless woman
next door, the patch-worked cat,

the man sliding his Penthouse beneath
the counter at the gas station—he wanted
to know about my nipples, rosy or dark?

I mentioned the dead. *They are communicating,*
I said, *and giving gifts.*

Years later, I had a nightmare. On a show
named Jeopardy I was asked to identify
the man on the ten dollar bill.

Another thing I could fail at.

This reminded me of sitting in a refrigerator, perched
upon the bottom shelf and how my grandfather
caught me, my head haloed with grapefruits

and Freon and light. He yelled at me
to protect the milk and the ham.

The words *curdle* and *rancid* shouldn't surprise anyone.

Again, the same church, beside
the same graveyard, collecting and disseminating food,
people, busy as ants, packed with a metaphysical weight
twenty times their own, all I know is that

my father will not be dead for another thirteen years,
my grandfather has just died, and a mistake has been made.
Alexander Hamilton was never president
and the date of my grandfather's death was engraved
by my grandma's name. I look
at my grandma's surprised face, see my own
and wait. This time we are awake.

Grave

October again,
and your body stirs, next to the magenta
flowers, a pumpkin, that gelato case,
waiting to be opened, dug out, scooped up.
How could I sit here and not think of dirt?
I carry your body everywhere,
even amidst the bright and sweet
of this grocery store's aisle.
Walk with me. See the muddied path we've left,
see how my fingers grip empty soil,
see how they won't let go.
My nails are crusted in my body's black mineral
and your ash, and this hollow dead space aches.
Haven't I carried you with me long enough?
Please. Go home.

Alone, I will lift the painfully red mum
up the steps to my new apartment.
Next week, I will watch its drooping petals
fall off, drop through me.
Like a vacant stem grasping
for its phantom limb,
I will reach for you.
I will hold on tight, I will begin to let go
of your holes you left me trying to sew:
a perforation in a vein, a fissure in a bone, all this
dead space. I will re-suture them with these threads
of days circling black on a calendar.

After three years, I am still the only
grave I have, still the only place I have
left to grieve,
to bear a flower,
to push away the scattered leaves,
to carve a name.

Bone Memory

Now that your vertebrae are misaligned
and the nerve pain pulses down your leg,
I cannot help but think of you, twenty years earlier,
lying on the worn brown rug of our old apartment
(the one we moved to when you decided to get clean).

I would sneak out of my room at night,
leaving the twin bed you bought for me at a garage sale,
to watch you sleep on the living room floor; a child's game,
I counted the ins and outs of your breath.

One would need more than my small hands
to add it all up. This child, her mother, two bodies
in one apartment with zero furniture, a hard floor
and enough money to buy only one bed.

Asleep on the hard floor, your body proved its love for me,
just as, the day I was born, when I pressed my bone head
against your spine and parted you from the inside,
you bore the pain of my existence, so that there would always be
a soft place for me to lay my head; your vertebrae,
a column of perfect white marble,
became less straight.

A Molar for Your Love

At first her lover asked her for small things. A hand to squeeze, for example, or a mint. And these she gave without hesitation. And then, after a few months of lying next to him, and getting up before the stars had left the night sky and watching the sunrise, and lying back down and getting up and so on. After a few months of that, her lover began to worry. Her body was not still enough, could in fact leave with the stars one night, was in fact returning only of its own volition. So one night he began to probe the inside of her mouth for teeth. He wanted more of a promise, a tiny molar would do, he thought. But after much deliberation he decided she might notice, might leave him then and not come back.

So he decided on an eyelash, an eyelash to make a wish. He plucked it, she stirred slightly and he made a wish. He wished that she would stop waking with the stars, he wished that she would stop rising, and that he would be safe. But once again, right before dawn, she rose and went out into the mist-covered grass and burgeoning pink sun, and exclaimed that the world was beautiful. This worried him a great deal. So the next night and the nights after that the lover went to work. Using strands of her hair he had begun to collect from the surfaces of his house and bed and body, he began to tie her down with hair knots as slight as his breath on her neck. Imperceptible restraints at first—she barely noticed the difference, just that it had become slightly harder to rise, harder to open her eyes.

Each morning she rose a little later, until one morning she missed the stars altogether. Instead, that morning she told him she felt the weight of a presence on her chest. He said it was just a night terror, just the myth of the Old Hag sitting on her chest. He said not to worry, he would be there to protect her from the ugliness of the world.

Answer to Why

The reason the plum is the same shape
as the human heart is the reason you ate mine
before you left without asking is the reason
I washed the pulp off the pit and pocketed it
to remind me is the reason I hid the next basket
with the stone fruit is the reason that ten mornings
together was enough it's nothing to cry over
is the reason you tried talking through my mouth
and I almost started letting you but grew tired
hiding is the reason I cut up my own last plum
threw the pit in the yard said the answer
was no when you asked if you could have it.

Saying Grace After Dreaming About Being Pulled Along the Niagara River, Even Though It Was the Size of a Creek and Held Very Little Water

Thank you subconscious or baby Jesus
for the holiday gift bags I found
in the riverbed. What a relief
to stop drowning and open presents:
a jar of slightly wet peanut butter
and a can of pork n' beans. Thank you
for that moment of reprieve from grasping
at the muddy shore, the disconnected
roots falling like hair shedding in my hands.
I realize my relief at seeing the gift bags
in the sharp rocks almost made me
forget: though I reach for the earth
it does not reach for me.

Motion Sick

I was five but the woman thought I was seven 'cause that's how old you had to be to be an unaccompanied minor, so that's what my daddy told me to say, so then I was an unaccompanied liar catapulting through the clouds and later I told my daddy, "I saw a lightning bolt," and he said, "Yeah, right," and I said, "Why?" and he said, "Cause I thought you said you saw an angel," and I said, "No, a lightning bolt," and we were quiet.

I was up in the clouds looking for angels and the nice stewardess offered me hot chocolate instead of pop, and maybe it was the turbulence or my open hands, but the next thing I know the scalding hot was all in my lap, and I was crying loud, but that's not the worst of it 'cause then I was standing in the front row butt naked from the waist down, just a simple small hairless vagina for all to see.

I was in the terminal on a layover, but I still thought every man I saw with black hair and a moustache might be my father, and I tried to go to them but the stewardess grabbed me back and said, "No, this is not your stop," so she sat me down on a chair and told me not to move and left me for what felt like hours and I had to pee so bad but I couldn't move 'cause I was still hoping that my daddy might surprise me and show up before his time.

I was chewing the bubblegum my mommy got me for popping ears when I started throwing up Dramamine and I might as well have been the plague or the grossest thing she'd ever seen 'cause the woman sitting next to me leapt out of her seat and pointed and said, "She's sick," which was true, but I cried anyways and then my new coat that had a detachable outer layer smelled like throw-up, so the stewardess put it in a plastic bag, which was the first thing they handed my father when he got to the airport.

Hubris

Once Bonnie made up its mind which way it would move, it didn't stop until it got there: Cape Fear, N.C. It moved ashore about 3 p.m. Wednesday, Aug. 26, 1998. Wind gusts reportedly reached 90 mph to 100 mph in parts of N.C., including around Wilmington and Wrightsville Beach.

          —excerpted from "Bonnie Batters N.C., southeast Va." in *USA TODAY*

After I tracked Bonnie's longitude
and latitude on the map for five days,
we watched the neighbors evacuate.
My father called it *a science lesson*
better than book learning when we loaded
up the generator in the back of his truck.
He said, *After we see the ocean, it's our job*
to keep grandma's meat from spoiling,
as we passed the cars lined up on the highway
in the opposite direction, and turned down
a dirt road to avoid the National Guard.
We stopped by the pier and the boarded up
surf shops, and stood ankle deep in sand
to watch the waves rise and the clouds gather.
My father raised his chin to the moving sky,
the wind blowing hard enough to make my ears ache,
but I could still make out his voice when he said, *Girl,*
after what I've been through, it'll take more
than a hurricane to kill me, and I was too afraid
to ask whether or not he was talking to me.

Back Before She Learned to Fly

running beneath the crab apple trees with a fist full of Wonder Bread. Back before she learned the word *no*. Before she traveled to the land of the *keep coming back* and the *it works*. Before she learned about happenstance and the happy dance. Back when tomorrow's *sorry*s were enough of a religion. She was a girl on the floor with cherry Pop Tarts and decoder ring dreams. She watched Bert and Ernie on the TV. Sitting between the rocking chair and the hard *knock knock* life. *Who's there?* A girl on the floor. A man in a rocking chair. A bird in a cage. A mama so mean that she'd kick you when you were down, looking at the floor, not making a sound. *Down down baby, down by the rollercoaster, sweet sweet baby, I'm never gonna to let you go.*

Packing

The half-empty perfume bottle, the broken-legged figurine
left to me in a will, they were all in the shape of unicorns.
This is how I inherited the paraphernalia of dreams.

First, I packed the unicorn puzzle, framed when I was three.
Next, the snow globe holding a horse with a white horn,
the half-empty perfume bottle, the broken-legged figurine.

Also, I found some letters and other things I had never seen,
like electrical circuits, carefully sketched, from before I was born.
This is how I inherited the paraphernalia of dreams

The letters home got shorter in the spring he turned nineteen,
and there is no one to ask about the medals gone from his uniform,
the half-empty perfume bottle, the broken-legged figurine.

Beneath the bed I found the Klonopins he hid from D—,
the dreamcatcher I made for his nightmares, and a box of porn.
This is how I inherited the paraphernalia of dreams.

Over the Atlantic Ocean he once repaired the radar system of an F16.
Now it all fits in the back of my car, the things I have left to mourn:
the half-empty perfume bottle, the broken-legged figurine.
This is how I inherited the paraphernalia of dreams.

Helium Dream, Post-Grief

You are ready to check out at the counter; the clerk approaches. He asks, didn't you want to buy a balloon? No, I want to buy these teeth, you say, cupping the tiny visible bones in your hands. He is confused. But I thought you wanted to buy a balloon? You look over your shoulder at the cluster of balloons floating on the ceiling, the shiny stretched material pushing upwards at a right angle to their strings. Distended bent necks, you think, helium would be everywhere if it weren't for these thin weightless containers. There are empty spaces in your head in need of filling. You feel the possibility of all the perspectives you can't pinpoint, and wonder what the clerk has seen. In your dream, you are everyone, even the girl behind you clutching a red string.

Bringing Water to My Father
While He Cuts the Grass

The grass is cold and wet and long under my toes
and he is fixing its length with a lawn mower,
trudging in rows and seeping sweat.

On his bare back the sweat droplets gather
like rain on cracked glass, as though they too are afraid
to touch the shrapnel scarred skin,
to reopen a wound.

I say that I am here,
but he doesn't hear me as I walk
behind him in his wake of perfect rectangular
grass patches with an offering of water.
The lawn mower roars past us in our separation

like an incantation that forces itself straight
through the thick hot air,
past my thin white wrists,
past the green tinted water glass,
past the ice cubes that vibrate and ting and shrink.
The water brims and overflows,

a kind of conductive meditation
and my finger bones hum
from the welcome cold. Just then
I reach out to touch him.
He snaps and turns.

There is a stranger writhing in my father's eyes,
and this strange man's hands are red
currents moving to encircle my neck.

And in this moment that I am this other man's daughter,
strangled, I see past the unopened spiral buds
of the morning glories, past the grass and the dirt.
I see their thick roots

that have begun to smother
the tendriled veins of the bearded
irises. The pale petals dry up and drop
one by one.
I see the worms, the sky, the rain, and the swollen stream.
I see all the miles over the ocean, the trees,
the red flame of a match he once told me he took to a leech.

I see the sound of the scream he makes when he's asleep on the couch,
as though such a thing could be seen.
I see his parachute opening.

The current of the Mekong River must have once moved a dead man's neck,
and the stranger in my father's eyes recedes,

ice water pooling and trickling around my toes,
and the pale shattered green-tinted glass
sits scattered over a perfectly cut patch of grass.

The Skeleton Pier

All this falling I saw in the Carolinas,
the summer the eye of the hurricane let loose
its calm, the red ants hunting for safety, biting
my sandaled ankles, remains—the dirt is sand here,
the house is still there, the pier is broken wood,
we're always shifting—dark grey bone-hard chairs,
the porch on which a bright green lizard froze.
Do you know there are companies that rent the beds
on which our fathers die? The metal frame and mattress
have been aired out and sent to the home
of a different dying man—
      We were surprised then, at all this falling,
even though it was the most certain thing—my father
teetering over the threshold, my shock at beholding him,
a skeleton pier, too tall and narrow to stand—
and this was all before the tumors moved, hinged
black masses on white spine and he would fall
down to the ground every time he rose—
      See the scene I replay, the restraints, beige
velcro, the complicated straps used to
hold him down when he wouldn't stop standing and falling—
standing and falling—*This is for your own safety*—
      Eyes wide, the same shade of coal as mine—
See the terrified ocean animal in him crawl
up to peer behind his eyelids, see it reach out
its deliberate strength and peel back each strap
trapping him down, see my chest bone cracking
open to show this hurricane heart still
circling hope—*Please, don't die…*
      Later, when the nurse came in and saw
the disassembled straitjacket splayed out
like flayed skin drying across a cannibal's hearth—
she said to me, *If you're going to unstrap him, we won't be
held responsible for his safety*—and when I tried
to explain that it wasn't me, she said,
It's not possible, he's not strong enough—

I should have said then that she had no idea
how strong we could be—the animal of my father's life
heaving itself over the metal bed frame.

It wanted to stand.

Bleeding Halcyon

My father wasn't that friendly.
My brother would never sit there,

since I don't have one, not really.
The space that he should occupy filled up

with too much fluid and our mother's desire again.
I am an only child with a skeleton boy brother.

This family of mine is not lit from inside,
but instead glows in the possibilities of Christmas nights,

and the years that will never pass
under the streetlamps on Street X. I thought I saw

my father's frown curling upward in the direction of a boy
that should have been my brother, that should have sat

next to me, our legs dangling off the edge of a porch,
like red flowers descending from the window box

of the first room. I would give anything to have
really seen his halcyonic skinned knees, the dirt,

an ascending worm,
the sanguine.

Inheritance

Nights I lay wrapped in the blue
and white Star Wars blanket I found in the shed.
I didn't care that it had been a hive's shroud, that R2-D2

had once served as a sarcophagus to a horde of wasps.
Their little carcasses had been brittle beneath my feet
when I disentombed them, crunching as loudly as the imperfect

peanut shells between my father's fingers at night.
The crisp black bodies were nothing that a washing machine
couldn't wash off the threadbare bronze and silver robot images.

Later, when my father lay dead in a cardboard box coffin,
I touched his skin, but heard nothing.

I left him to blister and splinter
alone.

Visitations

His mom used to say he had the neon disease.
When the lights came on, he woke up.
I, too, wake up to lights.
Last night before bed, I flipped the switch
at the top of the stairs to turn it off.
The light wouldn't go away.
Flickering, not like the gradual diminishment of a candle
flame, but like the persistent beats of a heart
that's unaware it's ending—more like the insistence
of the last words of a body
of a man who happens to be your father.
Green car, pretty wafer, daughter, daughter,
help me, please. Syllables dropping
like prayer beads. His last night
I was there resting my ears on the couch,
but his death wanted me
to stay awake for it.
I couldn't. Too young to have lain next to the end
of the end, and what was wrong with the wires
behind the fixture? Round face, tongue
of light, a ghost on the stairs. There is
no one alive to ask. When a light tries not to go out,
when a man who is your father dies,
when all you can think about are words
you didn't hear and that pillow,
the one he said he had, the one he said
you could always lay your head on,
when a light goes out and when you realize that
the safety of the pillow is gone, you wonder
what use it was to have been given
such a promise. You're alone now,
standing on a stairwell, watching
the light you turned off continue to buzz,
you're whispering to the dome fixture,
its flicker hanging on by a spark,
Father, die again if you want,
this time, I promise, I'll watch.

66

Double

I saw my father today
for the first time since his death.

He was walking toward the pillow aisle
in Bed, Bath & Beyond.

I followed him because I wanted to say
that I preferred soft pillows with a little bit of firmness
to those feathered pillows he always used to buy.

The plumes were always sticking into my skin,
as though they wanted to reattach themselves to
a featherless bird.

I was going to say, sleep shouldn't hurt so bad,
but he was holding a Memory Foam,
and I thought that was an improvement.

Playing Pool at "Taps"

At it again—it is Easter almost every night
but it is my father who is rising
in the back of the pool hall
that used to be a funeral
home. He is laid out, sometimes;
dead, sometimes; breathing,
sometimes; walking away
from his place in the cadaver
room to find me, sometimes.

I am the custodian of his ashes—
but tonight he is upright
and decomposing (I can smell him)
as a he presses a quarter down
onto the slate table and tells me
how very tired he is –

But I am getting better at this,
selfish daughter that I am,
resurrecting him more, not less.

Invocation to Ride

There was a Mustang made for two bodies that we called home.
We drove for miles on the highway, blinking and blinking away the distance.
I saw the white rectangles blur to a strip, a ribbon of time passing,

I said, I might take up smoking, it is something to do,
to pass the time, to end our time.

You died before I could tell you about the future,
about when I still did not smoke,
about how the white paint stopped its ribboning,
and we were still.

The Mustang became a picked over bone and you were a frame,
so I left you both.

I can be happy here, sitting alone, standing alone.
I have begun to walk slowly, to feel the way the gravel grinds
beneath my boots the same, the same as yesterday, the same as last
year, the year before all those years that I blinked away.

It is you who are different. It is you who have changed.
You are the dead man, and I am still one of the dying.

I follow the road, reaching out towards that rotating sky.
I listen to the air moving, the cells shedding,
but not piling up along the way. Even my memory of you moves
out like a ribbon. I am breathing a still noise. I am slowing.

If I die before I get to the end, lay me out on the movement of the lines.
Be still my cold limbs, my worn soles, my exposed toe bones,
and just let my tired body ride, just let it ride and ride and ride.

Exaltation

In the notebook I draw the eyelid
of your drawn face, I draw the reeds
rising up through the frozen pond –
I am moving away from what mattered –
I could go a whole day without touching
something warm—I am sorry to leave
us scattered—I said we were an exaltation
of birds because I wanted to hear you repeat
the word: exaltation—Exaltation for the people
with whom I have shared coffee or to those
I have touched roughly—Exaltation for the woman
whose face I passed on the sidewalk—I said
sometimes I look at people with a face flat enough
to set something on—You said I'm changing
the subject—I said there you go, setting something
on me again. And I show you my notebook, groups upon
groups of larks—They sing in flight, you know—
I look at you and the scattered feeling congregates,
the way a fine mist can turn into fog—the reason,
the radio says, for so much loneliness on the highway.

Seasons

Before Thanksgiving, at the Plains Indian exhibit, there were children
everywhere. One had a red scarf tied in a knot around her throat.

Was it me? Or did that mannequin baby look lifelike? When painting
pain, it's the depth of the folds in the skin around the eyes that matters.

Driving past the apple orchards,
the eyes of cows look lonelier to the lonely.

Remember last summer, the mosquitoes died so easily,
without a fight and very little blood. You looked like a rose.

Even in winter, there is light at the end of the day,
like a vague opening, like the first time.

What I didn't say was: "If it's a mechanism, I can break it."
You were discussing the involuntariness of breath and of love.

I've been thinking about all the bleeding girls in rest stops between
here and New York City. How many do you think are called Home?

My new sheets are pecan, my new candle, gold.
These are the ways I recreate the sun.

Today, the ice and snow thawed, the dripping of icicles
from the eaves sounded like fingers drumming on the bed post.

Little by Little

The man on the radio said, "There's a magical explanation for why the living die," and I thought of the dead moth I found on my bed. It was thicker than my thumb, its dark veins held still like rust, tendriling out against its golden bronze skin. The moth had often flitted about this moonish house, inching, little by little, towards my satellite lamp, its wings as delicate as a stream of water rushing over a washing child. I couldn't sleep.

Now it rests on my bedspread, a stiff statue, holding its winged shape. Somewhere in Texas, a man has taken a scalpel to the chest of a chupacabra. He is removing its bones, its eyes, its poisoned heart, and replacing them with straw and wire and chunks of glass. The chupacabra's dark leathery skin is all that is left to hold its mystical shape. Goat sucker, mange-ridden dog, in moonlight, when you haunted the back yards of our imaginations, did you know a secret alphabet? What would you have to tell us about the ways of man, about our proclivity to taxidermy, about why we think the living look so much better dead?

Michelangelo once held a chisel like a scalpel and said, "I saw the angel in the marble and carved until I set him free." What shapes would we find in the stones of water on the moon? We continue dying and killing and mounting our dead, higher and higher, making our way, little by little, to that lighted satellite. Have we confused the heights of our bodies with wings?

I will ask a friend, "Have you ever thought of the tiny worlds you destroy when you walk on the grass?" He will look at me startled, as though I had brushed up against him with a moth's wing. As though he thought there was no magic in that.

Patricide

When I ask my father,
who is pieces of bone and ash
in the green ceramic urn
on the bookshelf by my bed,
to forgive me for not killing him,

I say, I'm ready now, to kill you.

I ask his permission to reassemble his body,
to recreate his tendons, muscles, and bones out of dust,
to pull him out of the white-hot flames
of the funeral home's furnace,
lift his ninety-pound body out
of the cardboard box coffin,
and carry him home.

I say, Let's rewind time,

when I lay him out on the pale blue-flowered sheets
of his hospice bed, a womb of mattress and metal,
the morphine drip and feeding tube reattach,
snaking like an umbilical cord into the crescent
incision three-inches above his navel.
I put my hand on his skin,
thin and bruisable as the skin of stone fruit,
and feel for a heartbeat. He is a fifty-six-year-old dead fetus.

I say, I can't kill you, you're already dead.

And then there is a pulse,
his last slow-labored breath
exhaled and inhaled in reverse.
I want to wear the stench of his rotten gums
like perfume, his life-breath is so welcome.

I say, Let me bathe you one last time,

and I anoint him with Johnson's baby wash
on a soft pink washcloth. I had almost forgotten

the angular contours of the bones beneath his face,
and how I thought there was no more difference
between flesh and bone, his skin was so translucent.
Beneath the warm soft touch he coos.

I say, I wanted so much to please you.

I bathe his neck and his beating chest
with the heat of the pink cloth.
The tiny capillaries beneath his skin unfurl
their life-filled sails. I had almost forgotten
the way his stomach bile had erupted
through the hole in his abdomen, corroding away
the soft stomach flesh. Although I am gentle,
he whimpers. I remember why I am here.

I say, Take me back to a time before the pain,

and the abscesses on his backside fill in with flesh,
the burn from the stomach acid shrinks,
and the tiny black tumors uncoil themselves
from around his nerve roots, unclamping,
retreating, vertebra by vertebra,
to the smooth pink flesh of his throat.
He opens his eyes and looks at me.

He says, I had a dream I was driving in my green Mustang and you were there.

And I use my father's pocketknife to sever
the thick plastic feeding tube from its distended pouch.
The brown-tinted milky liquid flows over my fingers
and down my forearm; it drips
from my elbow and pools
on the carpet beneath his bed.

He says, Remember when you were a kid and I took you to the ocean.
You sat in the wet sand, digging holes with your hands,
looking for a shell that echoed.

I secure the little-red-plastic stopper
into the bottom of a morphine filled syringe.

74

He says, You wanted to take the sound of the ocean home with you,
but more water would come and fill in the spaces you had made.

I say, there was always more sand,
always another wave.

Beyond the sound of the waves
and the hollow of an urn,
I listen to the holes in the skin,
in the face, in the arm, in the heart,
in the space of his voice, losing his voice now;
this is the sound grief makes, not much at all.

Drawing the Mind

Mother, you know there is a place somewhere called Paris. It's a huge
place and a long way off and it really is huge.
—Cesar Vallejo, from "The Right Meaning"

When I was seven, I had a small chalkboard, a piece of chalk and an eraser.
At bedtime I used them to solve psychological problems.
I drew an uneven circle. *Mother, I said, this is you.*
I drew scribbles that waved and soared around her head.
This, I said, *is the problem.* I drew arrows coming out of her head,
going into her head. *This is how we'll fix you,* I said. *We'll think it through.*

Years later, I wasn't so hopeful. I went to New York, took a calculus class,
almost failed it. I went to Florence. I sketched a sculpture and then a man,
but didn't let him touch me. I wrote a poem. I scratched it out. I lay along
the side of the hill overlooking the Boboli Gardens and practiced rolling,
falling, letting go. I hurt myself.

In Trieste, I passed under windows of women in their beds
and calculated the time difference. I found a phone booth and called
my mother. I said, *Remember Buffalo.* I said, *Remember the night I called
the police. I remember,* she said. *And what about that time in the supermarket
when you forgot how to breathe? And the nightmares,* I said, *remember them?*
How we had them even when we were awake. You've got to take responsibility
for your own pain, she said. *Help me,* I said, and hung up.

In Paris, I went to the Modern Art Museum and saw Kandinsky's *Ambiguity*
up close for the first time. I thought I saw a two-dimensional representation
of an addict's brain with all its ballooning colors and shapes.
I thought I saw a way through it.
For the first time, I saw that an oval and a parallelogram could coexist.
I thought, not all the spaces have to be filled in, and syncopation is beautiful.
I thought, if you line up enough pieces together,
you can create something whole.
I thought, even a haystack can be disassembled, and that being
lost is only a frame of mind.

In the gift shop, I bought a postcard. On it, I drew a shaky circle.
I wrote, *This is me.*
I drew the rectangle of a coat collar.
I wrote, *I am tired of circumnavigating
the same pain.* I drew arrows going into my head,
going out of my head.
I wrote, *Mother, I'm getting better.
Look for me.*

Special Thanks

I'm so grateful to everyone who has ever encouraged me in my writing over the years; there have been many. I'd like to give a special shout out to Amy Hosig, one of my first poetry teachers at NYU, who showed me that this poetry thing was a thing. Thank you to all of my teachers and supporters at Syracuse University: Michael Burkard, Bruce Smith, Chris Kennedy, Brooks Haxton, Arthur Flowers, Dana Spiotta, and George Saunders. Thank you to Sarah Harwell for her wise words, and to Terri Zollo for sending the best emails. And thank you to my workshop cohort, Gina Keicher, Nina Puro, Kit Frick, and Andrew Purcell, and all of my other MFA friends for encouraging me and playing pool with me (Robert Evory and Ed Tato, I'm looking at you).

I'm grateful to Judith Kerman for believing in this book enough to publish it.

Thank you to Humaira and Charles for being such great friends, and helping me move from NYC to Syracuse to pursue this writing life. Thank you to Tate and Edmund for having had my back at various points in the drafting of this book.

I'd also like to thank my family: my mom, Anda Moore, my dad, Cliff Moore, and my grandma, Miriam Moore Smith. Thank you for loving me, and giving me pillows to lay my head on.

Note

In "Answer to Why," the phrase "the reason the plum is the same as the human heart" is taken from *The Possessed* by Elif Batuman.

About the Author

Devon Moore is a native of Buffalo, New York. She studied at NYU, CUNY Lehman College, and Syracuse University, where she earned her Master of Fine Arts degree in Creative Writing and where she currently teaches.

A former Syracuse University Fellow, Moore has also taught at SUNY Oswego, Le Moyne College, and Dewitt Clinton High School.

Her poems have appeared in *Gulf Coast, Harpur Palate, Meridian, The Cortland Review*, and others. *Apology of a Girl Who Is Told She Is Going to Hell* is Moore's debut collection.

Other Recent Titles from Mayapple Press:

Sara Kay Rupnik, *Women Longing to Fly*, 2015
        Paper, 106pp, $15.95 plus s&h
        ISBN 978-936419-50-0
Jeannine Hall Gailey, *The Robot Scientist's Daughter*, 2015
        Paper, 84pp, $15.95 plus s&h
        ISBN 978-936419-42-5
Jessica Goodfellow, *Mendeleev's Mandala*, 2015
        Paper, 106pp, $15.95 plus s&h
        ISBN 978-936419-49-4
Sarah Carson, *Buick City*, 2015
        Paper, 68pp, $14.95 plus s&h
        ISBN 978-936419-48-7
Carlo Matos, *The Secret Correspondence of Loon and Fiasco*, 2014
        Paper, 110pp, $16.95 plus s&h
        ISBN 978-1-936419-46-3
Chris Green, *Resumé*, 2014
        Paper, 72pp, $15.95 plus s&h
        ISBN 978-1-936419-44-9
Paul Nemser, Tales of the Tetragrammaton, 2014
        Paper, 34pp, $12.95 plus s&h
        ISBN 978-1-936419-43-2
Catherine Anderson, *Woman with a Gambling Mania*, 2014
        Paper, 72pp, $15.95 plus s&h
        ISBN 978-1-936419-41-8
Victoria Fish, *A Brief Moment of Weightlessness*, 2014
        Paper, 132pp, $16.95 plus s&h
        ISBN 978-1-936419-40-1
Susana H. Case, *4 Rms w Vu*, 2014
        Paper, 72pp, $15.95 plus s&h
        ISBN 978-1-936419-39-5
Elizabeth Genovise, *A Different Harbor*, 2014
        Paper, 76pp, $15.95 plus s&h
        ISBN 978-1-936419-38-8
Marjorie Stelmach, *Without Angels*, 2014
        Paper, 74pp, $15.95 plus s&h
        ISBN 978-1-936419-37-1

For a complete catalog of Mayapple Press publications, please visit our website at *www.mayapplepress.com*. Books can be ordered direct from our website with secure on-line payment using PayPal, or by mail (check or money order). Or order through your local bookseller.